ALL THE RHYME
Ramblings of a Rh
Farrell

All rights reserved.

No part of this publication may be reproduced, stored in a retrieval system, or transmitted, in any form or by any means, electronic, mechanical, photocopying, recording or otherwise, without the prior written permission of the presenters.

JM Farrell asserts the moral right to be identified as author of this work.

Presentation by *BookLeaf Publishing*

Web: www.bookleafpub.com

E-mail: info@bookleafpub.com

ISBN: 9789360940683

First edition 2024

ALL THE RHYME IN THE WORLD
The Ramblings of a Rhyme Lord

JM Farrell

India | USA | UK

To my wife Susan, may we meet again in another life.

To all of my family who have put up with my poetry readings, as well as some of the more dubious rhymes, without complaint for many years.

PREFACE

This collection of poetry and rhyme was written in various places, sat at the kitchen table, on the bus, in the pub or on a train to name a few, anywhere I can write down my musings or observations of the world. They represent all areas of my life as well as some frivolous fiction. People may recognise themselves within my work, please take it as a compliment, you are all my inspiration.

So, for anyone who has listened to the tapping on a screen on a bus, train or in the pub, this is what it was for. Please enjoy.

Owl and the Cat

Yes said the owl to the cat, I do think you are getting fat
The cat looked at the owl
With a frightening scowl
And said how dare you tell me that

You asked said the owl to the cat, and I know you wouldn't want me to lie
So I have told you the truth
And you've hit the roof
I am so pleased that cats cannot fly

The cat said I see, but I can climb a tree for I know that flying is absurd
And when I do
I am telling you
I'm going to eat you wise old bird

The owl said just think, there is milk to drink and you could try exercise
For it's easy to see
If you should eat me
You will just double in size

Thanks said the cat for telling me that, you are
very wise it is easy to see
For if I eat anymore
I won't get through the door
And it's fish we are having for tea

My Favourite Place

I walked along the beach
Watched the sun shining on the sea
Grey waves with foaming tips
Roaring as if calling to me

I watched the donkeys on the beach
With children in the saddle
As I removed my shoes
And stepped in for a paddle

I felt the sand rush through my toes
The water felt so cold
Smiling faces all around
Some young but many old

Then I walked along the pier
Spent coins in the arcade
I bought myself a whipped ice cream
And an ice cold lemonade

What an enjoyable day I had
I was spoiled, I must confess
I just can't wait to come again
To my favourite place, Skegness

Titanic

The hustle and bustle on Southampton docks
People carrying cases and checking the clocks
All so excited, some heading for a new life
Families all together, husband, children and wife
They were boarding the Titanic, a magnificent ship
Some quite apprehensive at this very long trip
They set off waving and cheering, shouting their goodbye
Just four days later so many of them would die

The rich on the upper decks, the poor down below
It depended on what you could afford, the way you would go
Edward John Smith was the Captain, a seaman so bright
So how could this happen on that fateful night
He had been told about the possibility of there being ice
But he was in a race and didn't listen to the advice
He just wanted to hold the crossing record
This proved to be something he could not afford
He should have listened to what was first said

Then maybe they would all have got there, and not ended up dead.

People were dancing and having such fun
Then there came a large shudder, the tragedy had begun
They had hit an iceberg at a very high speed
The water rushed in and would not recede
Don't worry said the crew, for this ship is unsinkable
The tragedy unfolding was simply unthinkable

Children were crying, mothers in tears
Fathers trying to comfort them, hiding their fears
The life boats were filling with women and children, mainly the rich
They soon filled them up, life is such a bitch
The poorer people travelling below
Found their way out blocked, and had nowhere to go

Credit to the band who kept on playing to keep folk calm
With no thought for themselves coming to harm
They let off the fireworks but it was all in vain
It was a very long time before any help came

The women sat in their boats and watched this great ship go down

And looked at the bodies floating all around
Men, women and children, tiny babies too
No longer rosy cheeked, for the cold water had turned them blue

It was a tragedy, so many died that day
And all around the world, the news spread with such awful dismay
Now this mighty ship lies on the ocean floor
With so many people who will be seen no more
I like to think their ghosts are still dancing and having a good time
And often wonder if this really was not actually a crime

Coward in Love

Whenever you are near it feels like a volcano
erupting inside of me
I would like to feel like this forever
But fear it will never be

All the stress and bad feeling I have are just
carried away on the wind
Can I tell you how I feel?
On this my hopes are pinned

If only I had the courage to tell you of this love,
if only I could be brave
But alas coward that I am
I just remain silent as the grave

The beauty of your eyes, your sweet scent, the
silkiness of your hair
I would like to hold you in my arms forever
But alas, I do not dare

If I could dispel these black clouds in my mind,
way up in the sky above
Tell you just how I feel
Tell you about my great love

What would I do if I could not see you, if you were not around
I must be brave and find the courage now
And finally stand my ground

Beauty Lies Within

It was a Friday evening
I went out with my mate
We saw two girls together
And asked them for a date

One was really beautiful
The other was quite plain
My mate, he got the beauty
I thought I'd missed out again

His girl's name was Kardy
My girl's name was Kath
Kath made me feel quite easy
And she really made me laugh

We took them to a restaurant
We didn't want them getting bored
Kardy ordered the best of everything
Whilst Kath asked me what I could afford

Kath wanted to know all about me
And what I liked to do
I heard Kardy say to my mate
This night isn't all about you

Whilst Kath was quite attentive
It soon became clear to see
When Kardy wasn't looking at her phone
It was all about me, me, me

Now I feel very guilty
It has put a huge dent in my pride
For now I know, you should never judge by looks
For true beauty lies inside

Get Yourself Behind Yourself

When I find jobs to do at home, but feel there is no rush
I remember what my father said:
Get yourself behind yourself and give yourself a push

You know that it needs doing, so don't you even think
About putting on your coat and going out for a drink
While no one was looking, I sneaked off to the pub
I had some pints of beer, and got myself some grub

Just as I started to enjoy myself, there came this awful hush
I thought I heard my father say:
Get yourself behind yourself and give yourself a push

So I hurried home and I got this small job done
I don't know why I didn't do it sooner, it really was quite fun

Now when I have to do the garden, I won't hide behind a bush
I will get myself behind myself and give myself a push

Shangri La

High up in the mountains is a place called Shangri La
Where the people never age, and never wander far
The air is unpolluted, the fruit hangs heavy on the trees
Animals live alongside humans, the people only want to please

They say you can only find it if you are pure of heart
The Buddhist temples in the mountains, that's where you must start
Just empty your mind and live every day as if it were your last
Never think about tomorrow, or long for what is past

Just enjoy every moment and banish every sin
Empty your mind of misery, only let happiness in
You will know you have reached your goal, after travelling so very far
Feel the peace and sheer contentment, there in Shangri La

Why God, Please Tell Me Why

Tommy huddled in the mud feeling cold and wet
Sitting with a company of men he would never forget
A picture of his family he carried next to his heart
Missing them so badly, hating the time they were apart

The men in the trenches, many of them smoking
Some of them crying, some of them joking
Most of them shivering from the cold or from fear
Thinking of their homes and all those they held dear

"Five o clock in the morning we start the attack
Orders are to keep going forward, there's no turning back"

Five AM, the whistle was blown and it was over the top
The enemy machine guns opened up, they just wouldn't stop
Men started falling, the mud turning red
Many of them wounded, many of them dead

Tommy was thinking of his wife and daughter
Would he see them again, could he get through this slaughter
Tommy kept going through this withering fire
But then got held up at the German barbed wire

He felt the wind from the bullets whizzing over his head
He had to make his way through, or very soon would be dead
At last he reached the enemy, opened fire like he didn't care
But he didn't want to kill, nor even wish to be there

That's when he felt the pain of a bayonet in his side
He reached for the picture of his family, then sadly young Tommy died

A young German soldier over young Tommy stood
Rifle in his hand, bayonet dripping with blood
He looked down at young Tommy with a tear in his eye
And whispered quite loudly,

Why God, please tell me why

Paul The Cat

I went out into the garden
And I saw this little cat
It was just a baby, or a kitten
If you would rather call it that

It was sitting on the grass
All on its own
It looked me straight in the eyes
I think it was looking for a home

I let it in the kitchen
And gave it a bowl of milk
I gently stroked down its back
Its fur felt just like silk

It drank all of that milk
Oh so very quick
I got some meat from the fridge
And hoped it wouldn't be sick

It rubbed itself against my legs
And didn't leave my side
Would I want the responsibility of this cat?
This was something I must decide

When I sat down in my chair
It jumped upon my knee
It just seemed to be so happy
Being there with me

I could hear this gentle purr
And then it finally went to sleep
Now I had this big decision
Did this cat I want to keep

At first I tried to find its owner
Then I took it to the vet
Yes, I bet you guessed it
I kept it as my pet

Now I heard that you can't train a cat
By the way I called him Paul
And he would always come back to me
When he heard me call

He would give me a special look
And he knew when I was sad
For then he would come and play with me
Knowing this would make me glad

He would bring this little plastic ball
And run it round my feet
Then dash into the kitchen
For his special treat

I just loved it in the evening
When I went to bed
He would jump up on my pillow
And lay just by my head

To feel his paw resting
So gently on my face
And see him looking so peaceful
Is something you cannot replace

He always liked to go outside
But never wandered far
But had this awful habit
Of sleeping underneath a car

He always came out when I called him
He was always quite alert
But then he had this awful habit
Of digging in the dirt

I believe his favourite time
Was when I was working in my shed
No matter what I tried to do
He would nudge me with his head

I had so many happy moments
With this lovely little cat
But alas their life is so short
There is nothing we can do about that

I woke up one morning
To find Paul was not on my bed
I thought he was sleeping in my favourite chair
But found that he was dead

I buried him in the garden
Where he had first been seen
I am sure that of all the lawn
That one spot is the most green

I hope there is a cats' heaven
Somewhere up above
For I know that he will be there
That little bundle of pure love

Jack The Squirrel

Jack the squirrel climbed the tree
So all around him he could see
Upon the ground he spied a nut
Laying next to a giant's foot

Jack scratched his head: oh deary me
I would so like that nut for tea
It's time for me, my wiles to prove
I will find a way to make that giant move
I suppose I could, just sit here and wait
But I am feeling hungry and it's getting late

So it was down the trunk so stealthily
Jack did travel down that tree
Then past the giant he did run
The giant shouted: this is fun

His face lit up he was full of glee
As jack ran back and up the tree
The giant looked up wondering what to do
Shouted: please come down, I won't hurt you
Come and live with me, be my pet
You will be nice and warm and won't get wet

Jack looked at the giant and sweetly smiled
For he realised this was just a human child
His mum will shortly call him for his tea
Leaving that nut down there for me

Never Alone With A Phone

I was sat in the pub when I heard these people moan
They said look at that man, he's here again playing with his phone
As I was listening, one of them said
He wants locking up; he's not right in the head

Now I knew this man, his name was John
I said hey up fella how are you getting on

He said I am on my own now, my wife passed away
And it's hard to find things to do every day
So I come in here, all on my own
If there is no one to talk to, I go on my phone

If only these people realised how lucky they are
Out with their friends and family, do you think they were going too far?
They should stop and think before they start to moan
For no matter how lonely you are; you are never alone with a phone

Day at the Zoo

There was Jamie and Lauren, Maddie and Lou
They went with their mummies to visit the zoo
Maddie said Mummy you must come and see
All of the monkeys are having a wee
Oh dear Maddie what can I say
All of my clothes are now covered in spray

Jamie and Lauren, Maddie and Lou
They all laughed so much that day at the zoo
They had a ride on an elephant, then a ride in a cart
They would have gone on the train, but it wouldn't start
Lauren said Mummy can we watch the llamas for a bit
Mummy said yes and got covered in spit

It's now time to go home, both mummies said
Get you your tea and put you to bed
They saw lions and tigers, crocodiles too
They had a wonderful time, that day at the zoo

How Must They Feel

How must they feel these young men returning from war
Their minds filled with sadness and friends they'll see no more
They will be asked, what did you do, where have you been
But so many will never speak of the things they have seen

They are quite unassuming, just one of the crowd
These are the people who make our country so proud
Occasionally you may notice whilst they are having a drink
A tear in their eye as they are starting to think

Of the bombs and the blood and their friends who were killed
Of the things they had done and the blood they had spilled
There will be things they have done that they will regret
And the horror of war they will never forget

They wake up at night from a very bad dream
They can still see the children, still hear them scream
How must they feel with all this in their head
They can never escape, not even in bed

So now is the time to say a quiet prayer
And thank the good Lord that you were not there

NEHEMIAH

On this certain day Nehemiah's brother came with a tale to tell
In the city of Jerusalem, all was not going well
The walls were pulled down and the gates had been burned
God's lessons to Moses still had not been learned

This upset Nehemiah so he went to cry and pray
He asked God for his help, and to please show him the way

King Artaxerxes asked Nehemiah why he was looking so sad
He told the King how in Jerusalem, things were really bad
Surely then there was proof, God had answered his prayer
For the King gave Nehemiah a letter of passage, to get him safely there

The journey was hard and long, his legs ached every day
Nehemiah he kept going, never forgetting to stop and pray

With the strength of his faith, and God hearing his prayer
Nehemiah travelled on relentless until he finally found himself there

The city's elders, at first, didn't want to listen; they didn't want to be told
But Nehemiah's letter from the King, soon had them all sold
He scoured the city in secret with friends late at night
The ruins pierced his heart; it was such a terrible sight

Nehemiah prayed to the Lord to help him to succeed
Then the people volunteered, all that he would need
All of the men and women some of the children too
They all wanted to help, for each one of them was a Jew

The walls soon started going up and so did the gates
This the Samaritans didn't like at all, and nor did all their mates
They planned to attack the walls and kill all of the Jews

But with the will of God, Nehemiah heard of this news

Then every worker with a sword was supplied
Each also had a guard, who stood by his side
It took fifty two days to hang the gates and finish the wall
They then went to the temple and prayed, God blessed them all

One man alone with his faith and the belief in his prayer
Had prayed for God to help, and the good Lord, as always, was there
Just an ordinary man, in esteem you couldn't hold higher
He did God's work here on earth,
This man was NEHEMIAH

Lucky

I got up this morning I was feeling rather down
So I put on my coat and went for a short walk
into town
I helped this old lady with a parcel; I carried it to
her car
The parcel was rather heavy and the walk was
rather far

This couple must have noticed what I had done,
I think
For they said; that was very nice of you, will you
join us for a drink
They both had a coffee and I had a cup of tea
Their names were Pat and Dave and they lived
in Grimsby

We had a great conversation, and then in the end
I had come out for a walk and made a new friend
As I continued my walk, I heard such an awful
scream
I turned around to see this little boy, he had
dropped his ice cream

He was being comforted, I guess it was by his mother
Then this lady behind the counter, came out and gave him another
I got home thinking about this and thought to myself, Ah bless
I am such a lucky person to live here in Skegness

No Lady, No

With her perfect legs and long black hair
A figure like a goddess, she wiggles everywhere
With just a nod of her head or a wave of her hand
These are the signals she thinks we should understand
With her Armani dresses and Louboutin shoes
She picks out the people she would like to use

But I say no lady, no, you can't have me
Because I am not the kind of man you would like me to be
Going out with you, I would find too hard to swallow
You are ugly inside, conceited and so hollow
You think, with your looks, you can have anything you see
But I say no lady, no, you can't have me

I prefer my women to be a bit more plain
Not so expensive and a lot less vain
You say that you want me and can take me far
Buy me nice clothes and a brand new car
Your beauty is your asset and your money the bait
You keep trying to tempt me to be your mate

But I say no lady, no, you can't have me
Because I am not the kind of man you would like me to be
So take your money, your looks and your car
And leave me alone because I know what you are
Go and find another man to temp and chase
Find someone else to take my place

Susan

I always told you that I loved you; I always told you that I cared
I remember the times we had together and the memories that we shared

I remember when I first met you, you changed my entire life
What a lucky man I was when you agreed to be my wife

I think about the wedding dress we got, it was the best dress we could find
I look at pictures of you in it daily; you are forever in my mind

When we first had our children I remember that look upon your face
Such happiness, joy and jubilation, I am sure nothing could replace

We always worked together; you helped me with all that I would do
You gave your heart and love to me, I owe everything to you

They say that for every man, there is a woman who is a perfect mate
Well you were that perfect woman; you were fabulous, just great

I thought that we would always be together, nothing could ever pull us apart
But then cancer came and took you and left me with a broken heart

If only I could feel your arms around me; your lips, your gentle breath
Nothing can keep us apart forever; I believe in another life after death

Born in the Wrong Body

I was born in the wrong body
This I want to change
Some people will accept me
Others think that I am strange
I was born a woman
But I want to be a man
If only people will accept me
The doctor said I can
I just want to be happy
And to change my life
I am living with a woman
We live as man and wife
I realise that a lot of people
Find this hard to understand
But I was born in the wrong body
Is this what God, for me, had planned?
I am not a great believer
Although it gives people so much joy
But if he's true, I am asking you
Why was I not born a boy?
When people look at me
Most will already have guessed
I have already had one operation
Doctors have removed my breast

So when we are having a conversation
Think about this if you can
I just want to be accepted
Please treat me as a man

If We Have A War

Man and woman were created for loving and caring
For having children, loving and sharing

We were not made to travel to far away shores
To interfere in their lives and fight in their wars

We don't live for long so enjoy your lives
For one day you will lose them, your husbands or wives

The loss is tremendous, the pain it is real
The emptiness and loneliness is something you feel

Interfere in other people's lives and you can be sure
Life will end sooner for some of us,

If we have a war

Bibble Babble Bobbit

Bibble Babble Bobbit set off to see the Slobbit
But on the way, he would have to slay, the ogre Slimy Gobbit
Willow Wood was Gobbit's home where no one dared to venture
But Bobbit knew, he must go through, to continue his adventure

Slimy Gobbit's name filled people's hearts with dread and fear
It was said he used your bones for bread, and drank your blood for beer
His teeth were green, he was unclean and he dribbled down his shirt
Unlike you, he didn't use shampoo, but rubbed his hair with dirt

Bobbit stood outside the wood, with his axe in hand
He shed a tear, for he had a fear, this could be his last stand

As Bobbit stepped into the wood, an eerie silence fell

The birds, they all stopped singing, then, there came this awful smell
Out into the clearing, with shoes that showed his toes
Came this eight foot smelly creature with a bogey on his nose

You must be Slimy Gobbit said Bobbit to this thing
I am off to see the Slobbits, to buy my girl a ring
I wish to marry Fanny and though soon I may be dead
If I manage to defeat you, it will prove my worth to wed

I don't want to fight you, Gobbit said, as he began to cry
All the things they say about me are nothing but a lie

They were started by my mother to keep people away
So that they would never see me, and have nasty things to say
Though I am very lonely, on the animals I can depend
I have rabbits as my companions, and the birds are all my friends

I long for human company, but it is clear as you can see
Apart from the fear, whoever came here, could never fancy me
Living here, in the woods, is such a lonely life
I wish like you, I could too, go and find myself a wife

Then join me on my journey, said Bobbit with a laugh
But before you do, I'm telling you, go take yourself a bath
Slimy Gobbit jumped into the water like he didn't have a care
He rubbed and scrubbed and cleaned himself, he even washed his hair

He really did enjoy himself, for him there was no turning back
That brook of blue, I'm telling you, was truly turning black
Bibble Babble Bobbit said look, I've cleaned your clothes
It's like a dream, you look so clean, now kindly blow your nose

They set off on their journey, towards the mountains of Morn

For just beyond the mountains, is where the Slobbits are born
The Slobbits are top class jewellers, known throughout the land
And Bobbit was determined, to get a ring for Fanny's hand

As they wandered down the valley, they came across a farm
You go first said Slimy Gobbit; tell them I mean no harm

The farmer had a daughter, a revolting girl named Pat
She was seven foot tall, built like a brick wall, and nearly just as fat
It was love at first sight for Gobbit, his heart it beat so fast
He said, I'm sure it must be magic; I've found someone like me at last

Pat wouldn't speak to Gobbit, she was very shy
She mumbled, uttered, and spluttered as she did surely try
At last she spoke to Gobbit, and this is what she said
My only friend is a pig, I am so big, I don't even fit in a bed.

People used to throw things at me; they used to make me cry
My father tried to protect me, and hid me in this sty
I am not a nasty person, I'm just misunderstood
It's just not fair, but they don't care, that I am living in the mud

Slimy Gobbit then did reply, he said your story's just like mine
So don't you see, if you come with me, everything will be fine

Bibble Babble Bobbit, who watched, standing with Pat's dad
Said, if you come and join us, it would make us both so glad
Pat thought about it for a minute, as she had to think it through
She said, yes I'd like to come, if Harry can come too

Now Harry was a great big boar, which you know is a male pig
And just like Pat and Gobbit, he really was quite big
So with the farmers blessing they set off again once more

They were sure they heard some cheering,
behind that farmhouse door

In the mountains lived some bandits, with a
reputation they had earned
For many people had entered here, but none had
yet returned
Some say that they are cannibals, and eat
everyone they see
So don't go into the mountains, or they might
take you home for tea

Bobbit was a small man, with two giants by his
side
Followed by a great big boar, big enough for
him to ride
As they entered the mountains, one hundred
bandits did appear
But this small group of travellers, they did not
show their fear

Pat said; don't try to stop us, but the bandits they
did try
So then Pat spit, and she hit, their leader in the
eye
Slimy Gobbit thought this was really, all just so
much fun
And when the boar began to roar, the bandits did
all run

At last they reached the Slobbits, and Bobbit got his ring
Everyone was dancing and the birds began to sing
The Slobbits were gentle giants, and Pat and Gobbit quite fitted in
In fact, in the land of Slobbits, Pat looked rather thin

The Slobbits invited them all to stay and make this place their home
Pat and Slimy Gobbit would never again be on their own
But Bobbit got on Harry's back and the journey home began
He would give the ring to Fanny and prove he was a man

For Bibble Babble Bobbit, the journey home was long and hard
But he got a warm welcome from Fanny's mum, and Harry a bed in her cosy yard
Fanny came out to greet him, with a great big smile
Bobbit hugged her tightly; she'd been on his mind for such a long while

Bobbit showed Fanny the ring and said, just you name the day
I will promise that I will never again, leave you or go away
Harry was at the wedding, although his feet were sore
But when they exchanged their rings, you should have heard him roar

Fanny was so happy she was the perfect wife
Bobbit knew, her love was true, and they would have a happy life
This was an incredible journey, one Bobbit would never forget
He now has his beautiful wife, and a very large family pet

Oh What A Challenge

Oh what a challenge this has all been
There will have been better, that they will have seen
But it hasn't stopped me from having a go
I could possibly fall lucky, you never know

I have so many ideas going through my head
Even at night whilst I'm laying in bed
I will put on the telly, just for a short while
I like something light hearted, to make me smile

Then an idea comes into my mind
That I have to write down, always in rhyme
Sometimes it's political, sometimes it's rude
Sometimes it's funny, but it is never crude

I write so many rhymes, nearly one every day
Am I going mad, will they take me away?
The things that I think of might make me smile
Like the old smelly giant and rocking crocodile

I am so pleased I saw this challenge; I suppose it was just luck
As it gave me this opportunity to put some poems in a book

ACKNOWLEDGEMENT

There are so many people that have inspired me over the many years of writing it would be impossible to name them all and if I've missed you out, I apologise.

Firstly to my dearly departed wife, Susan, for your love and support to the end, and to my daughters Vicki, Jacqui and their husbands Chris and Rob for your love and patience, and a bit of editing support. You have all listened to my ramblings with a smile or encouragement along with my grandchildren, Lauren, Jamie, Maddie and Lewis.

Thanks also go to my lifelong friends and family at home and abroad and to new friends made along the way, you have all been my inspiration.

My faith has helped me through my darkest days along with those at St Paul's and The Storehouse, I thank you too.

I can't finish without acknowledging the team at BookLeaf Publishing and their #TheWriteAngle challenge for providing the opportunity to publish my work.

Milton Keynes UK
Ingram Content Group UK Ltd.
UKHW020837050624
443777UK00015B/482

A collection of rhyme and poetry from the mind of JM Farrell in his observation of life, love, loss and all things weird that make you smile.

You are invited to enjoy an exploration into the mind of a Rhyme Lord.

ABOUT THE AUTHOR

JM Farrell is a widower who, when not travelling or spending time with friends and family, enjoys putting his thoughts in rhyme. From fun rhymes and religious rhymes to children's stories, memories and rhymes of love and loss, he writes constantly.

Born and raised at the seaside, JM draws inspiration from the location and visitors as well as family, friends and his faith.

Occasions are celebrated with personal rhymes, often wild or wacky, but always full of love and the recipient's character.

Following the mantra that everything can be solved with a cup of tea, JM can be found with a cup whilst writing. Just don't forget the sugar.